Fragments of the Dawn
and
Other Poems

Fragments of the Dawn
and
Other Poems

E. O. LEBLANC

Copyright © 2025, Edward O. LeBlanc

All rights reserved.

No part of this publication may be reproduced, distributed, or transmitted in any form or by any means, including photocopying, recording, digital scanning, or other electronic or mechanical methods, without the prior written permission of the publisher, except in the case of brief quotations embodied in critical reviews and certain other noncommercial uses permitted by copyright law. For permission requests, please address Picard Press.

Published 2025
Printed in the United States of America
Hardcover ISBN: 978-1-7376126-2-9
E-ISBN: 978-1-7376126-3-6
Library of Congress Control Number: 2025902427
Picard Press, New Jersey, USA. picardpressinfo@gmail.com
Cover art by Aaron Hamilton
Cover design by Stacey Aaronson
Book design by Giselle Laurent
Translations by Gregory Rabess

"Fragments of the Dawn" and "Vade Mecum" were previously published in the 1968 Edition of Important American Poets and Songwriters by Valiant Press. The poems in this volume are offered by the heirs of Edward O. LeBlanc. All works are either reflections on the author's own experience or are fictitious. In certain cases, names and identifying characteristics have been changed to protect the privacy of specific individuals.

Edward and Ethel LeBlanc
(circa 1965)

In honour of a legacy that endures,
and a life whose grace continues to inspire.

TABLE OF CONTENTS

Foreword i
Introduction 1

Section I
  The Unstableness of Things..................... 8
  Far Away 9
  The Lost Chord 10
  Fragments of the Dawn......................... 11
  Fragments of Thought.......................... 13
  When Love Is Gone 14
  Pots and Dots.................................. 15
  Life's Philosophy............................... 18
  The Gamut of Life.............................. 21
  Do You Remember............................. 23
  Vade Mecum 24
  To The Ambitious Youth 29
  The Living Paradox............................ 32
  Daniel's Bane 33
  What Would You Do? 36
  A Lover's Message............................. 38
  A Lover's Thoughts............................ 40
  Acrostic.. 42
  What You Will.................................. 43
  The Place Where I Was Born................... 44
  Ode to the Bee................................. 46
  The Storm...................................... 49
  Sundelia—An Introspection.................... 50
  Towards West Indies National Song 52
  The Little Eight 53
  A Tribute to My Teacher 55

Section II
    Fortress of Hope: Voices Against Injustice 59
    Nomn Nwè 60
    Black Man 61
    Cièck La Vie 64
    The Cycle of Life 65

Epilogue 75

Acknowledgements 77

The late author's words, kept unchanged from a privately printed collection in 1967, for the poems in Section I.

FOREWORD

Dear Reader,

It is with diffidence that I trouble you with these badly expressed imaginations of a youth when your time could be better occupied with some illustrious novelist or poet whose works you had read before.

The circumstances which impel me to take such a daring step, I hope, may urge you to read—not for information but amusement, although these hackneyed lines could hardly aspire to such distinguished honour.

In perusing the worn-out pages before me I am obliged to identify that youth as having once been myself, and even if I were to prune from, or add to, what is presented here, I am not equal to the task.

Therefore, I have preserved the order in which they were written so that you may follow, step by step, the sequence of thought as the youth gradually grew older and more mature.

Finally, I uphold the division of labour—the youth has written. I am transmitting it to you; you will, dear reader, take your share of responsibility to read and criticise.

*   *   *

The first part of this foreword to these verses, with the exception of the last three which were composed at a much later date, was written in 1947. Today, twenty years later, I am reluctant to dispense with it in favour of an entirely new introduction since it makes a specific point about the earlier compositions which I started at the age of seventeen.

"Fragments of the Dawn" and the prize-winning poem "Vade Mecum" appear in *Important American Poets and Song Writers* printed in 1947. In the case of the latter, only a small part appears in the Publication referred to above since I had to conform to the rules governing the competition by not submitting a poem with more than thirty lines. Thus it was also necessary to reconstruct the two opening lines and to transpose the stanzas.

I wish to make special mention of Mr. Ericson Watty for his invaluable suggestions and Mr. Alick Lazare for his kind assistance in reconstructing some stanzas in the earlier poems.

Edward O. LeBlanc

INTRODUCTION

I first came across this collection of poems (Section I in this collection) on a shelf in the St. Mary's Academy library while completing my last year at high school in 1969. I remember that moment clearly, so original and fresh were the poems contained therein. The collection had been printed by the Dominica government printery earlier in the 1960s, during a period when Edward LeBlanc was launching a cultural renaissance encompassing folk traditions in music, dance, song, and story-telling, as well as encouraging poetry, short story writing, and drama. A spirit of nationalism was in the air, and a diverse array of creative citizens were joining the movement with great enthusiasm. Edward Oliver LeBlanc (1923-2004) was not merely the national leader but was the inspiration behind this cultural revolution, serving as Premier, Chief Minister, Agricultural Officer, and poet.

Born at Vieille Case (some would more specifically say at Reposoir, near Penville) on 3rd October 1923, LeBlanc was educated at the Vieille Case government school and took a course in Agriculture at the Imperial College of Tropical Agriculture, Trinidad, in 1944. He later studied on his own for the London Matriculation Certificate obtained in 1948. He worked in the civil service as

Agricultural Instructor (1945–53). He then was employed by the Dominica Banana Growers Association (DBGA) as agent in the northern district. During this time, he served as nominated member and then elected member of the Vieille Case Village Council. In his spare time, he wrote poetry, some of which was published in the US and most of which is presented here in this book.

In 1957 he joined the Dominica Labour Party (DLP), which had been founded two years earlier by Phyllis Shand Allfrey and E.C. Loblack. LeBlanc contested the general elections of that year and won the Portsmouth seat in the Legislative Council. The following year he resigned his seat to contest the federal elections and, along with Phyllis Allfrey, was elected to represent Dominica in the Federal Parliament of the West Indies, led by Sir Grantly Adams of Barbados. Allfrey was made Minister of Labour and Social Services. She was already a published poet and novelist with a literary following in England, marked by her best-known work, *The Orchid House*, a book that fictionalised her childhood and foretold of her future political activities on the island. Besides politics, this interest in literature created a bond between her and LeBlanc. But strains in that relationship began to appear from 1960 when LeBlanc resigned from the Federal Parliament to contest the local Dominica general elections of 1961 and to blaze an independent path. He led the DLP to its first victory, winning the Roseau South constituency and becoming Chief Minister and Minister of Finance. In the aftermath of the collapse of the WI Federation in May 1962, he participated in all of the conferences in London and Barbados, attempting to save a federation of "the little eight" islands, which were left after Jamaica and Trinidad went independent.

Finally, when all else failed, he attended the 1966 Lancaster House Conference in London to make Dominica a self-governing Associated State in March 1967 and became the island's first Premier. Already in 1965, he had changed the longstanding colonial holiday, 'Discovery Day' on the 3rd of November, to National Day, and worked with poet and lyricist Winston O. M. Pond to create a national song that is now our National Anthem, with music by L.M. Christian. The key to understanding all of this is rooted in the background and character of LeBlanc himself.

Born in the north and later working as an agricultural extension officer in the east and west of the island, he knew more than most Dominicans about the island, the people he led, and the conditions under which they lived. (In 1966 he was elected as representative for the Western District Constituency, centred on Colihaut.) Above all, he had a passionate belief in Dominica and things Dominican as only those who are intimate with this island can have. His skills of communication with 'the little man'—in the field, at the bayside, in the street, in the rum-shop—became renowned. These associations were in many ways his greatest strength.

The reasons for LeBlanc's great popularity were clear. Although most of the roads and social programmes financed by the Commonwealth Development and Welfare (CDW) funds had been planned, and in some cases begun, before the DLP took office, it was during the period of 1961–66 that they were completed and bore fruit. The DLP was identified with these achievements, and a prize-winning Kwéyòl song celebrated the road to the east coast with the words:

Anou haylay hooray!
Anou haylay bwavo!
Chimen wivay Au Vent, Au Vent,
Labour ba nou chimen!

Let us shout hooray!
Let us shout bravo!
The road has reached La Plaine,
Labour gave us the road!

But historically, there were two even more basic reasons for the success, from which everything else resulted. The first was that never before had there been such a surge of development concentrated at one time upon a people who, for generations, had lived at subsistence level at the mercy of social and political conditions over which they had had no control. The second was that LeBlanc and the Labour Party had presented them with a form of leadership with which they could identify, speaking in a language and presented in a manner they could understand.

By 1973, however, LeBlanc was becoming weary of leadership. Faced with protest demonstrations over another attempt at regional integration, this time with Guyana, he was also dealing with conflicts with the opposition Dominica Freedom Party, as well as with the Civil Service Association (CSA), supported by other trade unions. The country life of farming, fishing, and family was beckoning, and he felt that it was time to hand his trail-blazing mission over to younger members of his government. In July 1974, after over fifteen years in public office, thirteen of which he had led the country, Edward LeBlanc resigned from politics. In April of that year, he was already hinting at his departure in an interview with the *New Chronicle*.

> 'Though I accept and welcome change, I myself can't change too much, that is why people said that I was "Black Power" and this and that.... When we returned and got the constitution in 1967, I let it be known to my party that I will remain for only two terms, and after that they will have to get another leader. In a democracy at times, the sort of pressure you get, people sometimes not being sincere and what not, you tend to react, and when a leader starts reaching that position it is not good for him or the country.'

LeBlanc was being accused of autocracy in his manner of dealing with the opposition, the unions, and even with members of his own executive. The rising dissension in the country, his previously stated views on the subject, and family considerations led to his resignation announcement on 26th July 1974.

The position of Premier went to Patrick R. John. LeBlanc retired to his seaside home at Vieille Case at the early age of fifty and withdrew completely from public life, except for one occasion when he joined a bipartisan delegation in London, to negotiate the island's independence from Britain. In retirement he offered an open-door policy to primary and secondary school students in the area, who wanted to learn, interview him, or access his library and archives for the occasional school project. He died at his home village on 29th October 2004.

Today, his poetry provides us with valuable insight into the mind of the man, much deeper than any political and social commentary or biographical assessment from the outside could achieve. This collection is a creative treasury that reflects Edward LeBlanc's voyage through a life filled with transformative action and personal reflections, spanning the middle of the twentieth century, and giving a very personal meaning to those most significant years of change in the history of Dominica and the wider Caribbean.

> Dr. Lennox Honychurch
> *Historian, Anthropologist*

Section

I

The Unstableness of Things

The forms of life are ever changing,
Each day brings a different world,
Nature is always re-arranging
What the transforming world unfurl'd.

Today brings joy, tomorrow sorrow;
No one's happy every day,
And each today is each tomorrow
Mentioned every yesterday.

The span of life so brief, so fleeting—
So short for those whose lives are good!
Time moves past sees Time retreating
And Age creeps up where youth had stood.

Yet Time moves on too long and slowly,
For those whose lives are filled with wrong,
Then strict requittals for their folly
Make their lives seem much too long.

Our neighbour's cares we ne'er consider,
Save when stern Experience rise
And block our bright and happy pathways—
A sorrower learns to sympathise!

Far Away

Far beneath the distant clouds
I see a line 'mid sea and sky,
'Yond which my groping eye can see
A little home—a paradise!

The din about me fills my ear,
The crowd around me blocks my way;
Too many things for which to care,
My mind is drawn so far away—

Far on my little island home,
Where my desires all prevail;
For in that paradise alone
Dwells that angel of my love.

The Lost Chord

Hands clasped in deepest adoration
The children as they pace the aisle
Sweetly chant in ardent supplication
"Oh, come and mourn with me awhile".

I see the form of my departed Joyce
With them; I listen, but in vain.
I'll hear no more her tender little voice
Piercing through the sweet refrain.

Fragments of the Dawn

PART I

The little meadow all around my door
Welcomes my half-awakened eyes;
And Nature's pets, frolicking as of yore,
Fill the air with many joyous cries.

The lovely flowers just waking up from sleep,
Embalm the air with all their fragrant hue;
They kiss the sun while for their joy they weep,
For through the sun they feel refreshed and new.

The swaying trees enjoy with mirth and glee,
The change of time from night to light of day,
And with their blades they wave each sister tree
Which, in return, replies the same old way.

Corollas with their petal mansions bright
Admit the little birds that cross the streams,
Which then return the pollen cushions light
That change the maiden blushes of their dreams.

The little kittens, welcoming the day,
Peep at themselves with understanding eyes;
They lift their paws in form to say good day,
And stretch themselves to chase their sleepy sighs.

But Nature all in one sweet blending mood,
Begins its task to get the days work done
And aims to get the work complete and good
Before the brightened spark of daylight's gone.

Fragments of Thought

PART II

Amid this bond of unity refined,
Man sometimes tries his worthiness to show,
But he so crammed with vice and hate combined,
Attaineth not that natural fruitful glow.

In man lies treach'rous Hate, and hate is sin,
And born in sin remaineth prone to sin;
Thus prone to sin he hates his man of kin
And makes this world a place of constant din.

And man, so blind to all that Nature teach,
Allows himself to curse, to fret and lie;
Concerned with things that lie beyond his reach,
He lets the golden moments pass him by.

Such moments rich pouring at his poor feet
Whate'er or where sad man may ever be;
But he so crammed with conquest and defeat,
Pass by the things he's then too blind to see.

But like a breath of unseen air they fly—
These transitory objects of our day;
Yet Nature's works will never fade or die
Though those who pay them tribute pass away.

When Love Is Gone

When love is gone, and all its charms are gone!
Sweet lips, soft words, warm smile and tender touch,
It robs the heart of all its pleasant thrills,
Denouncing lips and all their faithless vows,
Replacing space for flesh in the embrace,
Confounding all!—warmth, sweetness, tenderness!
Fulfilling all they promised in reverse—
Deceit for truth, sorrow for happiness
A burning hell for promised paradise—
We pine, we fret, because the sting remains
Tormenting, goading, painful torturing
Yet hov'ring round the periphery of thought
We soon forget its sorrows and its pains
And muse on all its sweetness once again.

Pots and Dots

Softly in the moonlight clear,
Reclining on their canvas cots,
Were Hyram and his cousin fair,
Discussing little Pots and Dots.

With mocking words they laughed and joked;
Their harmless gossip flowed along
Until they found that they invoked
Strange feelings which grew very strong.

But ere the drowsy moments flew
That mark an hour's space of time
Their joyous gaiety changed anew
To something deeper and sublime.

And like the dawning of new days
The moon of love on them did shine
Lightening Dots' innocent ways
Revealing Pots' am'rous design.

As Pots and Dots had no more spots
To occupy their fickle tongue
Like children shameful of their thoughts
They raised their voices in a song.

Their voices softer, sweeter grew,
And though their notes were in discord

The more they sang the more they knew
Their yearning hearts were in concord.

And then their voices sang no more
But like the billows, closely crawled
Nearer and nearer to love's shore
In the other each enthralled.

Fond Cupid left his arrows charms
In those hearts so close-combined
And in four eager longing arms
The cousins found themselves entwined.

Was it their fault if, unrelenting,
Their kindred blood their sense dissolve
Transforming all that harmless fondling
Into inevitable love?

Could they avoid the unforseen
Or could they tear the links apart
That form the chain of love, or screen
The loud vibrations of the heart?

But ere the juicy nectar flew
From their avid lips and tender
Sneaking realisation grew
And broke their loving hearts asunder.

Th' emotions reason did subdue
And forced them to forget and part
But the after effect I knew
Would be two broken ruined hearts.

But that a lesson to them taught
(For then they blushed while on the cots)
Blame not others if they're caught
Behaving just like Pots and Dots

You who read this please refrain
From asking me of Dots and Pots
Because I'll ask you in same strain
Tell me, who are Pots and Dots?

Life's Philosophy

The span of life of every man
Is but a modicum of time
Which flies as swiftly as it can
To regions lower or sublime.

But each and everyone in turn
Must stand upon this worldly stage
To act his part ere he returns
To greet his proper heritage.

Back to the dust from which he came
Man is embraced by mother earth,
But high aloft his spirit's flame
Will brighter burn as it goes forth.

'Twill go with trembling fear to hear
What other life it has to face
Is it to be the place so dear
Or hell's great torments and disgrace?

Whate'er the goal that he doth meet
Was made by him and him alone.
The surest guide of his own feet,
He was the maker of his throne.

The lasting heritage of the soul
Is built on faith and self-denial

He, to achieve the highest goal
Must with true patience meet each trial.

Vain pride can never ope' his door
Dull hatred never meets his heart
But good and helpful to the poor
And kind to all he plays his part.

The thoughts of lust he drives away
He meets adultery with disdain
But as a neighbour he holds sway
In soothing those who suffer pain.

There is no falsehood in his heart
On his lips no perjury lives
He keeps the bad and good apart
In his creator he believes.

And greed adorned in golden want
Was chased away before he spoke—
He is not vain, but truly valiant
That smiles under his heavy yoke.

Luxury to him is a disgrace;
Pleasures useless vain and vile
He looks the whole world in the face
For in his heart there is no guile.

He'll reap the fruits of his good toil,
He will enjoy the golden home,
He has maintained his lamp with oil,
In happy paradise he'll roam.

The man who thinks this world is all
Remains his passions' constant slave,
Lower yet he has to fall
Disgraced in a disgraceful grave.

His thoughts all bent on worldly gains—
Ambitions pregnant with excess,
And hatred, greed and other's pains
To him are pleasures and success.

Intemperance his only guide,
All choked with lux'ry, vice and pride—
The gate of life he stands outside
The house of death he sleeps inside.

The faithful man forgives and grieves
By love and faith his actions driven,
The poor pretender ne'er forgives
And may not hope to be forgiven.

The Gamut of Life

Of all the stages life contains
Each has its share of anxious thought,
Although we seldom entertain
Debasing deeds that we have wrought.

But Reason walketh up with Age
And Conscience guides the hearts of men,
While sad Remembrance lights his rage
To bring life's gamut in its ken.

Things that besmirch the life gone by
Man ne'er is prone to contemplate,
And though the good he may decry
The time will come to ruminate.

There is a spot in th' heart of man
That's always ready to repent,
Which has a force much stronger than
The strongest mortal can prevent.

And at the time when life stands forth
Between the streams of youth and age,
His childhood life he would betroth
Yet grasping at the adult stage.

But as each day must yield its place
On to another coming day

The wanton years of younger race
   Emerge into a stricter play.

The years which once could never end!
   They live as short as shooting stars,
And aging life doth time befriend,
   Thus grappling closely with its fears.

And like the billows roaring on
   In close succession each to each,
So years and days in common run
   Do hasten to the aged beach.

And so the 'teens to twenties yield,
   And thirties, forties, fifties frown
Upon life's old untrodden field
And leaves the past an empty crown.

But ere the heavy gate of sense
   From its abode away is cast,
The thoughts recall against pretence
The scattered memories of the past.

Which—scattered memories—when rejoined,
   Become a chain of endless strife
   Combining all the past to form
   The honour or disgrace of life.

Do You Remember

Do you remember, dear, when we first met?
That lovely night you kissed me at the door?
That, I'm too weak darling to forget,
You've got me dear to love you more and more.

Just one kiss from your sweet tender lips,
One thrilling moment in your loving arms,
Just one smile upon your gleaming cheeks
Brings life to me with all its pleasant charms.

You brought me thrills when first you kissed my cheek,
You stole my heart when first your lips met mine,
You stole my voice for then I couldn't speak,
Now you to me mean love and life divine.

When you look bored it fills my heart with pain,
When you look gay 'tis all I wish to see,
When you are cold, I wish a kiss in vain,
When in my arms, the world belongs to me.

Vade Mecum

Beneath a clouded unseen sky—
The distant can'py of this world
Where only a curious star would pry
Before it found itself uncurled,
Sat I upon a little mound
Strewn with flowers all around,
Gazing thoughtfully with sad eye
Upon the crowd that waddled by
With white sticks, similar to mine own,
Burning mournfully at one end,
Flickering the more the lesser they had grown,
That I embraced the mound I did attend.

With sorrowing eyes and painful fears
On the beginning of myself I dwelt—
Which I knew not—though I shed tears.
But how, or why, I never felt
Maybe, 'twas for the Joy of seeing light,
Or the infant's sudden fright
When extracted from its dim abode
To adopt a new and unknown code,
Or for reasons which I can't explain.
Loosened, my thoughts slowly mounted
Th' incomplete ladder of my life
And dropped to where the earth was mounded.

Encircled with flowers that little mound
Assaulted by nature's ceaseless tears,

Its shape lost, had almost reached
The level of the common ground.
The common ground bearing all
My joys—the object which I love.
Now covered by the powdered stone
Rotting e'en each tiny bone.
"Rest thee here my love" I cried
"Till we meet on th' eternal train"
And though to repress the drops I tried
I began to weep again.

"Is it my fault if like the streams
Meandering on their constant course
Into the wild and wavy ocean,
Forever filling where there's much,
Draining the poor to enrich the rich
My tears should fall upon that spot
Like a cascade unto its bubbling base
Feeling the pangs of an early loss
That can never be replaced?
Ah yes! His will be done
But though I know it I still must weep
Because my dearest, sweetest one is gone".

With such restless thoughts pouring in
my mind
And the heavy beads bearing down my cheek
I scarce observed the fewness of the lights,

For others like their carers had dispersed,
Save a deep mourner like myself
Then pacing wantonly away.
"Should I depart and leave her there?
She who cared for me both day and night
For two hundred moons and over?
Should I be so base and forgetful
And deprive her of what she would desire?"
No, I could not—I lingered there.

And linger there I did until I slept,
Till I heard her voice, much like the days
When she woke me at dead of night
To heed dame nature's bidding
Lest I did them where I slept.
A voice so charming and so sweet
That I listened to the music of that voice
Before I answered—"Mother!"
"My darling son" she said "Come with me,
I'll escort thee to thy father's home
For I dwell not here alone
But always at thy side."

"But Mother" ventured I, and ere
I could say another word she said:
"My son, I see thee always, and thou
Hast done, as I would have thee do.
I know thou lovest me, but such a love

Exists for me alone. Cherish that other one
Which has lately grown in thee,
For the love I taught thee in thy youth
Was a mere foundation to build upon
A pure celestial love, of which
I most willingly approve.
Now must I part—another comes
Cherish her, she's thy true love".

Alone I stood—she disappeared—
And wondering who should come.
For one brief moment, tranced in expectation
My heart refused to budge
And left me like a lifeless shell
Deserted by its occupant.
But was it long? I could not tell,
For there she was—a frame of loveliness,
Not only prettily pure but purely pretty
In her long white robe.
And like one being in the compass of four arms
We were tremulously entwined.

Must I go on, with use of earthly words
To express a joy so harmoniously divine?
Can mere words describe such an embrace?
Or explain the sweet delight
Derived from such a kiss?
I can only say that ere I knew, myself,

I was alone; save for Phoebus who,
Peeping from his oriental home

As he began his diurnal tour
Over that section of the earth
Explained it all to me,
And with one long look
At the illegible epitaph
I sighed—and went.

Is that enough? Does it explain
That those I met were those I loved before?
I apologise if my efforts are in vain
But with one request that you may see
And try to feel the way I do;
Two loves—both inevitable
Each with its share of joy, preceding its portion of sorrow.
The one by natural circumstances
The other by sudden inspiration,
I can't forget the one
Or cease to love the other.

To The Ambitious Youth

You who are gifted with ambition's flame,
And if that flame is all that you possess,
Keep it burning with the fuel of fame,
That brightened paths of great men to success.

Allow not fame to be your special aim,
Use just its flame to guide your groping thought,
Success that only harbinger of fame,
Will buy you what for others it has bought.

Many try and make themselves succeed,
But many also fail to reach the end,
Through lack of faith in studies to proceed,
Or some "good friend" their failure did portend.

Or just because the lure of happy time
Was stronger than the law of abstinence,
Or that the fruitfulness of thoughts sublime
Could not be reaped without the help of pence.

The path, though blocked with stone or barbed rail
May be crossed with method and precision,
If at the first and second steps you fail
Let your failures be an inspiration.

They learn best how to achieve success
Who have drunk the bitter cup of failure,

For failure in itself is a success
If it enhance the hope for better future.

Be the trustful master of yourself,
Let self-respect and courage be your guide,
Sully not your name with vice or stealth,
But possess, not vain, just manly pride.

To get one thing you must forego another—
Each satisfaction an alternative.
Do not let your mind relax and blunder
But make your aspirations positive.

Finance cannot foster true ambition
And lack of it should not bring you dismay,
Once there's a start pursue your inspiration
Nature daily demonstrates the way.

Disregard the jeers of casual friends
Who may think your hopes beyond your realm,
Let thine own self upon thyself depend
And with thine own hands hold and guide
the helm.

Do not be daunted by criticism—
It shares a common source with jealousy,
Let not vile talks invoke defeatism
But prove your mettle with true decency.

You may be laughed at if you ever fail,
But please fail not to try and try again,
He who ne'er tries may not expect to fail
But success he cannot hope to gain.

Yours is the crown if only you would seek,
More great the strain more bright will be
the gem,
If you in all you do are strong yet meek
Your own will be the priceless diadem.

The Living Paradox

Disguised in formal and ostensible power
Holding the sparkling sceptre and the helm
Magnanimous man maintains his rigid rule
Serving the wily woman's will
Believing that that power is all his own.
He rages war—if woman says he must—
Against his bosom friend: His hottest blood
Soon curdles when he sees the artful tear,
She knows it too, that cunning's an endowment
All her own; and that no sound lasts longer
Than the echo of her silent kiss. She rocks
The little cradle, the mighty world she rules
Remaining still in fondling innocence
The paradox of this prodigious world.

Daniel's Bane

The days of four and twenty years he'd seen
Loving each lovely dame with thoughts to wed
Each in her turn becoming a HAS BEEN
Forgotten as his fickle fancy fled.

Once, indeed, he took into his head
The hopes a lovely lady's love to win
His love for her with full confession spread
But she misjudged sincerity for sin.

With bastard failure meeting his first move
He found no pleasure in the singing springs;
With old infatuation did he rove
Shielding his heart from love's disturbing stings.

Alas! Did love become a jest to "D"!
He lightly felt, but very strongly pressed
His love for all indiscriminately,
Indulging passion's passionate behest.

Watching one day the little shattered school,
Where once he spent his irresponsible years,
He spied a lass commanding with good rule
The little kiddies seated on the chairs.

Her voice had brought enchantment to his ears
And left him spellbound in a magic trance.

You'd think he nourished Bed'vere's joyful fears
Or was transfixed by Arthur's glitt'ring lance.

That lass so young! A blushing bloom of youth
Untainted and untouched; and so demure,
Appeared to Dan the epitome of truth
And all that's truly, wonderfully pure.
Said he:
"I watched her long, discussing with myself
Her beauty and her form. Her eyes so fine!
I watched and praised. Then that mischievous elf
Turned their soft light directly into mine.

"I blushed, and blushed again against my will,
But then I saw the blushes in her eyes
And all the things that once to me were still
Began to echo sweet melodious cries—

"The wind was music, the birds began to sing
Across the skies I saw a soaring dove
It was fairer than the fragrant dawn of spring
When I beheld my first and only love.

"Oh! Those long hours I watched her seemed forever
While musing on a future life of bliss
In taking for my own that dainty flow'r
Oh! how I longed for her delectable kiss.

"Having to put my courage to the test
I thus approached to speak my inner thought
But ogling half in earnest half in jest
I only hovered round the central spot.

"And so the moments swiftly flew away
Leaving the thoughts unsaid, the deed undone.
With heavy heart I watched the end of day
Marked by a solemn disappearing sun.

"Unknown to me love drove me like a goad
Finding myself in presence where she was—
The way of love's a labyrinthine road
And love's abode a maze of corridors.

"A thousand schemes I laboured in my mind
How to relate the havoc Cupid wrought
But found no speech in words of any kind
To speak the simple message of my thought.

"Alas! When I found words to tell it all—
That which I wished to say and which I knew
She longed to hear, I saw her eyelids fall
The life was gone which no love could renew."

No further could he go with his oration
As trembling lips explained his grave distress,
And the ling'ring tears of perturbation
Drowned the emotive words he would express.

What Would You Do?

If you were rich with wealth beyond your needs
And shone with glamour, glory, pow'r and fame,
With each day bett'ring the one that it succeeds
    Adding sumptuous titles to your name
        What would you do?

    Our life is just a short but timely tide,
    Our wealth is but an instrument of pride,
    In order that His wish be not denied
    Dame Charity should be your lawful guide.

Were it your lot to be among the poor.
With nought to eat or drink when you desire,
With abject misery knocking at your door
Making you wish from this world to retire,
        What would you do?

    Patience is a virtue free to us all
    And faith is all the life of every soul,
    Your low estate is just a heav'nly call
    To sublimate for the celestial goal.

Or if you did in virtue dwell down here
With nought to force repentance on your heart,
Living a life that knows no earthly care
Waiting from this heritage to depart.
        What would you do?

Success depends on how much you impart
By constant efforts to your weaker friends,
If you are rich in virtue and teach not
Before 'tis late begin to make amends.

Or were you a mere compact heap of vice
Unable life itself to dignify,
A prey to all that fetch a fatal price
And being vile you others vilify.
What would you do?

Reliance in yourself is all you need,
Your worth still lingers in potential stage,
Command your will your stumbling steps to heed,
And nurture you to sit among the sage.

Or were you nursed by wisdom's cultured hand,
Or wading 'neath the heliconian deep,
A member of the esoteric band
Distinguished: for respect's not all you reap.
What would you do?

Cease not endeavour. Add upon your score
If scoring be to teach what you have scored.
If you teach not, you are not wise but poor
For wisdom is the fear and love of God.

A Lover's Message

When the shades of night are falling
And your cares of day are gone
When dull sleep to you is calling
And maybe you're all alone
Watching the lamplight
As it flickers bright
Or doing nothing
Your loving heart singing
Do you think of me though far
And wish me near to you
Holding you tight in my arms dear
And your lips upon mine too?

Or can you hear my lowered voice
Calling you, darling, all the time?
(Wishing I could make the choice)
Saying you always will be mine.
Or as we're far apart
You would have the heart
To forget me cold and calm
And greet another in your arm
I hope you're not pretending
And if you're always true to me
(For each day my love is growing)
And you mine alone will be—

One day, darling, one day
I hope not very far
We'll ban all cares away
At our marriage fair.

A Lover's Thoughts

To you my dear this message comes
From my heart sincere and true,
And I hope that it becomes
A timely balm for me and you.

The clock has struck the midnight hour
And I alone am up from bed
Reading harder than of yore
But, dear, you're always in my head.

I've laid the tattered book aside
Only, dear, to contemplate
Of what may be the future tide
That'll crown or mar our happy state.

And as my pensive thought takes wing
Darling, I think of only you—
Of your sleep which goes unending
Oblivious of the world you knew.

Ah! You cannot think of me my dear
You're too happy in your sleep,
Yet I'm glad you have no care
Though, of course, I cannot sleep.

I see you, yes, I do, my love!
The very heaving of your breast,
Just like a winsome carefree dove
That sleep has brought to thoughtless rest

Though I know you sleep so sound,
I have one wish—(a little beam
Brings it always round and round)
To be always in your dream.

So dear, you see love's endless care—
Sleep, dream, heartache, unrest.
Goodnight my love; stern sleep I dare
Though I'm tired and long for rest.

Acrostic

Excellent lady for her virtue praised
　Unequalled in her love and tender care
　　Ne'er uttered one uncouth debasing phrase
　　　Or frowned if others chanc'd to scoff at her
　　　　Mother of a dozen of her own
　　　　　In whose joys and fear she played a part
　　　　　　Expressing mother's love with mother's care.

Oh that such a piece of nature's art
　Lovely pattern of a mother poor
　　Indeed she lived and loved and played her part
　　　Valued all; to all she ope'd her door;
　　　　Even she is gone and feel no more!

Let me not weep the four short decades you
　Enjoyed down here and wish you had stayed more
　　But wish that you enjoy the life that's true
　　　Lounging at the foot of your creator.
　　　　Alas! I wish it, yet I wish you here,
　　　　　Near to me to cheer my sleepless brain
　　　　　　Come, mother, my peace of mind restore.

What You Will

When in the Kingdom of sweet silent thought
And governed by remembrance of you dear
I marvel at the pain and pleasure brought
By your presence which is ever near.

The tender message in your farewell note
Left sweetest joy inside my heart of pain,
And though I know you mean just what you wrote
I always have to read it once again.

To hope to see you dear on your verandah
Is a daily routine task of mine;
I pray the Fates all hindrance to debar
That we can woo each other all the time.

The Place Where I Was Born

Young is the night!
But with graceful equi-languid strides
Dame Diana in her magic splendour
Slowly strolls across her room to spread
Her irridescent mantle o'er the glade.
The owl hoots in some far distant shade
The little stream still murmurs o'er its bed
And each repeats the sound that went before,
All with one unwritten law abide
To make the night full bright.

Those joyful screams!
Which I am able now to muse upon
Graced the night three hundred moons ago
When my weak involuntary cries
The first noise I made upon this earth
Joined the chorus of this natural mirth.
Those sounds can only meet me now with sighs
For I am sadly grieved that things are so—
The mother's gone the way of flesh, the son
Is left with dreams!

I hear the fife
My uncle played to make me sleep when I
Was yet a child. I remember all!
Yet no evidence remains save
The shattered remnants of a two by four
With trees and grasses for a floor

Ah that she were here! She who gave
Me all and hearkened to my every call!
Ah! Would she were here to smooth the sky
O'er my discordant life.

Ode to the Bee

The world awakens! And slowly throws away
Her garb of night, and as slowly decks
Herself with variegated hues to greet
The radiant sun—the grave yet cheerful monarch
Of the east—whose sparkling jewels sway
The dawn clouds with instantaneous checks
And dart their meteoric rays to meet
The mountains in a rainbow-coloured arc
And warn the lazy moon.

The silent breeze now whispers through the pines
And all the bushes echo with its tune
As it gambols through the labyrinthine
Carpets of the verdant field. The sunny
Hill-tops shiver in a haze. The vines
In tremulous silence, form a pale festoon
For painter Phoebus to incarnadine.
And all the birds compose a symphony
Of many melodies.

But you, noisy drummer of the dawn—
Poised on buoyant wings with your unique
Melodious hum—surpass all in aim
And constancy. 'Tis true you pillage all
The flowers that you greet, and having drawn
The nectar'd sweetness from each cup, you kick

Upon the bosom of your host and claim
The very dust within to cram
Your communistic realm.

You pay the cost of what you feed upon;
For what are you but cheerful lord whose
Presence presages fertility
Be it on the hills or in the valleys?
Your daily work is never fully done!

But what of it! You make your daily cruise
And no blame can be yours. A certainty
It is: you never deviate from the alleys
Of nature's policies.

With envy I observe your happiness
Waving your leafy winglets o'er the glade!
You torture me for all the painful joys
You bring; for now, you soar to aimless heights
And now, alas, with eagle-falcon swiftness
You sweep down beneath the sleepy shade
And cheat my pensive eyes—Those mocked toys
Which subject all their other natural rights
To your vain caprices.

Perchance you've gone and left me to my lot
To marvel still upon your graceful trick

And heat my fev'rish brain. But here you come,
Crammed at the back with powdered
yellow dust.
Ah! What pleasures you enjoy! Soft!
Are you gone? and whither? am I sick
Or have you lulled me to a sleep that some
Men ne'er enjoy? Or did I dream?—I must
Have courted sweet repose!

The Storm

The sky was grey, the clouds were thick
Flash followed flash
From dawn.

All life so scared while nature bawled
Bleat after bleat
Forlorn.

The rain still poured; the sea enraged
Blast answered blast
Till morn.

The storm had ceased so out we went
Each private loss
To mourn.

Sundelia—An Introspection

What have I been?
A lovely maid contented and in peace
Adorned with Carib jewels of one kind
Neatly fitted on my sturdy breast.
'Twas peaceful then!
The Spaniels came
Subjected me to ruthless exploitations
Against my own consent. Defense I tried,
But failed. Almost all my jewels lost
That's how I fell!
Before they went,
Not contented with their valued spoil
They some base metal by the jewels left.
With boastful pride and flaunting flag
To Engle went!
Young Engle came
To claim his share of my invaluables
And like his predecessor, all agog,
Boasted to licentious Franc
Of ownership!
A fight ensued
Now wife to Engle or harlot to old Franc
I became. Fight followed fight! Franc failed!
And I remained young Engle's servant maid
I who was queen!

Slave trade
Brought Africans to my trammelled bower
Whether I would or not and I became
Concubine to them all. I was weak
Might was right!

What am I?
But mother to all colour class and creed
Nurse to Gentiles and to Jews. Harbouring
All ideas that relieve or plague the world—
Franc's sentiments!
Engle's pride!
Spanis' partiality and Afric's discontent!
The red man's obstinacy inconstancy and
slyness!
Not omitting the wanderers' avaricious traits
Yet I'm none.

What'll I be?
Indeed what can I hope to be? Soon
Mars may ask for interplanetary law
And yet I'll have no place,
No culture
and
No creed.

Towards West Indies National Song

Our loyal voices join in chorus,
With hope and love united stand;
Prepared to build—with God before us—
Th'West Indies, our native land.
Let all West Indians to the fore
Uphold our nation's name:
Our motto's based on motives pure,
For justice, not for fame.

Fostered by need for strength and freedom
Our scattered isles our cause acclaim.
Holding hands, we, by His wisdom,
Solidarity proclaim.
Our banner, bold, aloft and free,
Unfolds our common cares.
Our link, the Caribbean Sea,
Will bind us through the years.

> "Our natures do pursue,
> Like rats that raven down their proper bane,
> A thirsty evil, and when we drink we die."
> —Shakespeare, Measure for Measure, Act I, scene II

The Little Eight

Veneer eroded, the corium shows,
Exposing stark reality—
Brutal, naked, unadorned!
Humanity dehumanised,
Principles undefended,
Moral hopes confounded,
Rights denied.
And lucre reigns supreme—
A harbinger of mercy
Mercilessly applied.

The strong unite, the wealthy join,
The poorer to divide and rule.
Eight small sticks, together bound,
Confirm the parable of old:
Disregarding size or length,
With full co-ordinated strength
The job is done;
But otherwise, must face
Ultimate destruction
Taken one by one.

The days of auction blocks recalled,
The fight for freedom, unabating,
Transcendent through the transient years
Goes on. Our progenitors.
Both enslaver and enslaved,
Had freedom on their hearts engraved.

"Hold on! Hold on!"
(re-echoed from the past)
"Your destiny to mould."
Victory will be won—At last!

A Tribute to My Teacher

You are gone! Time may perchance
Dispel the memory of a life
Which shines along the path of those
You shaped and moulded on the anvil
Built on truth and discipline:
I can't forget your patience whose
Endurance was an inspiration.

I may forget your stern appearance
Which veiled a kind heart (like a shroud)
That all selfish motives spurned:
But can't forget your understanding
Which was, in fact, a revelation
Of what, in modesty, you sought
To hide from public scrutiny.

I may forget the gems of wisdom
You taught me, which kindled my
Desire to appreciate
The mystery of life: I can't
Forget 'tis mean to revel in
Pride in victory's exhaltation—
For that your teaching did impart.

I may forget, in one weak moment
To conceal the fact that I
Performed a goodly deed for some
Deserving soul: but I'll remember

Your philosophy—'the giver's doubly
The receiver. No one does
Enough who does not do his best.'

I may forget that self esteem
No ally is to self defence:
I shall remember that his acts
And not his words proclaim the man.
I may forget a lot you said—
Or did: but I'll remember you—
Your humble unassuming self.

And when the day-to-day dull care
Do yield to memories of the past
I shall remember you as teacher
Guide and confidant and friend
Whose good advice could smooth the rougher
Edges of despair—To you Adieu
God's blessing be with you.

Section II

Fortress of Hope: Voices Against Injustice

Why waste your breath on this enchanted isle
To teach your kind what mankind ought to know—
Where harshness reaps a kind and friendly smile
While love, deceit and hatred sow?

Enchanted! Yes! With nature's carpet spread,
With foliage and flowers dyed with dew,
But where the poor must live in fear and dread
Under a vocal unsympathetic few.

Can you succeed where others would have failed,
And break the tyrants' rod, the poor to save?
If so I shall proclaim (as I have hailed)
Your message, though it makes the tyrants rave.

And when the curtain falls and all is done,
The pathway cleared and all obstructions flung,
We'll see the goal illuminated by the sun
And hand in hand will keep the fortress strong.

— Written by E.O. LeBlanc in 1961
courtesy of Lennox Honychurch Archives

Nomn Nwè

Nomn nwè ki léchèl? chimen
Ou té ké vlé pou'w swiv
Pou'w wivé denmen
Kèl vi ou vlé pou'w viv
Pou'w waché
Déwasiné
Détwi
Tout jennman yo mété an tout chimen pawan'w
Ki tjenbé-yo é ou dèyè jik jòdi?

Katjilé byen, pis
Tinni sitèlman chemin
Adan, gwan, étwèt
Glisé oben woché
Men chonjé
Ki lalé
Ki lawi
Ki twas
An tan pasé ou maché san katjil
Ou pa katjilé'y, ni twasé'y, ni fè'y.

Magwé lanmen'w mawé dèyè'w toujou
Lidé'w lib! Mé libèté ni pwi!
Was-ou é wasin-ou sé pa joujou
Enmé tout, men enmé was-ou pli

Black Man
ENGLISH TRANSLATION

Black man, which road
Would you wish to follow
To reach tomorrow
What life would you live
To uproot
De-root
Destroy
All obstacles put in the paths of your progenitors
Which have kept them and you behind until this day?

Think well because
There are so many roads
Some wide, some narrow
Slippery or stoney
But remember
Be it lane
Be it street
Be it track
Formerly you walked them without thinking
You did not plan them, nor trace them, nor build them.

Although your hands are still tied behind your back,
Your mind is free! But liberty has its price!
Your race and roots are not things to play with
Love all, but love your own much more

Twavay wèd
Padonné
Pwiyé
Lowizon'w klè, koupé chimen'w ou menm
Evè kouwaj pétwi dèstiné'w.

Work hard
Forgive
And pray
Your horizon is plain, cut your own road
With courage, your own destiny to mould.

Cièck La Vie

Manzè Sabrin assiz douvan kabé'y
Ka katjilé signifikans lavi
E sa i dékouvè an lidé'y
Pou nou sé yon fòmidab filozòfi.

Chivé gwenné, tèt blan sé kon koton
Plat pyé'y flijé, lanmen'y plisé
kadav-a'y masakwé o baton
Mé sèvèl-li ovif sé kon dasyé

Zyé'y klè ka pèsé kon pikwa
Tout dan'y si fò, èvè si byen plasé
Ki pèsonn pa ké kwè ki vyé fanm-la
Té sa tini yon san é senk nanné.

I ka pansé kouman lavi chanjé,
E an menm sans lavi sé kon sézon
Ki ka chanjé men ka viwé wéglé.
Menm biten men diféwan wézon.

Nati sé menm, lapli, zéklè, lowaj
Koul van, plézi, lapenn, ka pété fyèl.
Bèl klè zétwèl ka dispawèt an nouwaj
Sòlèy toujou wéglé pa jou an syèl.

Tou lé nanné pyé bwa la ka fléwi
Gwenn ka tonbé, viwé pousé ankò.

The Cycle of Life
ENGLISH TRANSLATION

Ms. Sabrine sat before her hut
Contemplating the meaning of life
And what she discovered
To us, is sound philosophy.

Nappy hair as white as cotton
The soul of her feet cracked, her palms wrinkled
Her body crushed to the extreme
But her mind was as sharp as a sword.

Her eyes clear and piercing like a pickaxe
Her teeth so strong and evenly lined
Defied anyone from realising that the old lady
was a hundred and five.

She is wondering how life has changed,
But yet realises that life goes like the seasons
Which constantly change but remain constant.
Things don't change! The reasons do.

Nature is the same; rain, lightning, thunder,
Storm, pleasure, heartbreaks seemingly
    unbearable.
The brilliant light of stars dimmed by clouds,
The sun makes his diurnal tour of the heavens.

Every year trees flower,
Seeds drop, and again grow into trees.

Siwen toujou ka tombé lannwit
Pou asiwé ki pyé bwa-la pa mò.

Lé zanimo, miyon, fawouch, sovaj
An pak, mawé, oben ki lib an bwa
Pwéson gwo dlo, an wòch oben an vaz
Zwézo anlè, yo tout anba menm lwa.

Tout nonm, tout fanm anba lwa-la osi
Zanfan ka fèt, ka pofité, ka mò.
Zanfan-yo ni pou fè menm osi
Tout chimen ka bout a menm lapòt.

Kan i té jenn, jenn fanm maché touni
Pis moun an sé tan-la té inosan
Jòdi wòb kout anpil moun ka fwéné
Latè-nou la jòdi otan méchan.

Avan sé zèb anmè èvè penpen
Mé moun té fò, yo té ka viv pli lonng
Jòdi sé fonmaj, bè tab èvè pen
Mé lavi kout, sé pawòl-la ki lonng.

Avan, moun pa té tini djè pawòl
Mé yo toujou té ni bon santiman.
Jòdi yo ni pli vwa pasé siyòl
Men mové tjè yo ka fè yo chè manman.

Dew falls in the night
To ensure that the trees do not die.

The animals, tame, wild, ferocious,
Caged, tied or loose in the woods
Deep water fish, in stony or weedy areas
The birds of the air, all observe the same laws.

All men and women are also under the law
Children are born, they grow and die.
The children repeat this refrain
All roads lead to the same place.

When she was young, young women walked
 naked
Because people were innocent in those days
Today short dresses cause some to shiver
Our world today is terrible.

Long ago, it was bitter grass and breadfruit
But people were strong, they lived longer
Today it is cheese, table butter, and bread
But life is short, it is the recounting that is long.

In the old days, people did not talk much
But they were always of good disposition.
Today they are more vocal than the Kalinago wren
But their hard hearts still ensure a mother's love.

Tout tan sé menm, men toujou diféwan.
Mistè sala nonm pasa déchifwé'y
Sa koumansé dépi an tan Adam,
Ni zèb, ni flèv, ni gwèv pasa chanjé'y.

Evè tout katjil-li i pasa inyowé
Ti manmay-la ki ka jwé an sab-la,
ka pwan on kokwiaj pou'y benyen
Pa èvè dlo men èvè sab chèch-la.

Vyé fanm-la fwémi-kéchoz boulvèsé'y
Zyé fizé'y anlè é bwa kwazé
E dékouvè on piti ti klèté
Ofon lowizon tjè-a'y té ka kléwé.

Magwé si vyé, si las, si mètwizé
I vwè on lison an ak ti manmay-la
I vwè was-li ka fòsé, twibilé
Dépi latè kwéyé jis jòdi-la.

I vwè tout parantaj ansyen'y maléwé
Ki pasé douvan avan'y
Tout chimen I menm pasé é tini pou pasé
Chenné, swèf, bwitalizé, é fen.

Every age is the same, yet always different.
This mystery, man cannot unravel
That started since the days of Adam,
Which neither obeah, flood nor strike can change.

With all her thinking, she cannot ignore
The little child, who is playing in the sand,
Taking an oyster shell to bathe
Not with water, but with the dry sand.

The old woman shivered—something shocked her
Eyes fixed upwards and with folded arms,
She discovered a very little light
Beaming deep in the horizon of her heart.

Although so old, so tired, so emaciated
She learned something from the action of the child
She saw her race straining and harassing
Since creation to this day.

She saw her progenitors impoverished
Who walked before her
All the roads she herself travelled and still must travel
Chained, thirsty, molested, and hungry.

I vwè gwan, gwan, gwan...papa'y
Déwasiné hòd péyi nati'y
Kon plan yo ka waché é wiplanté.
Maléwé-la kité lonbwi'y pou bon

I vwè papa'y anba lingwèz béké
I vwè manman'y anba tout kalité baton.
I vwè sésé'y pwan tout pèz dan kwazé.
Yo soufè tout—yo pa té sa di non!

Yo simé, fouyé, planté, sèklé, wékòlté
Swé laswè fwèt an solèy plen midi.
Do yo touni, douvan yo pli mové.
Péché-yo—koulè-yo pou mèt-yo té pini.

Men tan kon layvyè fò ka lavé nèt
Nou pwan tè pawan-nou senyen pou-la
Jòdi tab-la touné, nou menm sé mèt-nou.
Laswè-nou sé pou nou jan plas-la.

Vyé fanm-la vwè tout sa an vizyon'y
I vwè kò-a'y sé kon yon pon an lò
Ka jwenn tout jénéwasyon-a'y
Kon sèk san bout pou koumansé ankò.

She saw her great, great...grandfather
Uprooted from his native land like
A plant pulled up and replanted
The poor man left his navel for good.

She saw her father under the white man's grip
She saw her mother molested and raped.
She saw her sisters bear all strain with clenched teeth.
They suffered all. They could not say No!

They sowed, plowed, planted, weeded, reaped
With cold sweat under the mid-day sun,
Their backs naked, their front in a less enviable state.
Their sins—their colour which deserved punishment.

But time, like a flooding river scours clean
We now possess the land our parents bled for
Today the tables are turned, we are our own masters.
Our sweat will be for our own advancement.

The old woman perceived all this.
She saw herself like a golden bridge
Joining all her generations
Yet again like a hoop without end.

Nou ka konpwann mèyè pasé avan
Nou k'ay twavay ansanm pou pli pogwé.
Ni jenn, ni vyé, ni mal, ni savan,
Pyè Donmnitjen pa ké sa igwété.

Nou tout, annou pou National Day-la,
Chanté, dansé, wakontwé, an hod vwa
Tout pou chak, chak pou tout
Konsa, tout tan, tout Donmnitjen ké ni yon vwa.

We understand better today than before
We shall work together for further progress.
Neither young, nor old, nor indigent, nor sage,
No Dominican shall have regret.

Let all of us, let us for National Day,
Sing, dance and recite with loud voices
"All for each, each for all"
So that, all Dominicans will always speak with one voice.

EPILOGUE

E.O.'s anthology is a delightful after-dinner treat, filled with questions that invite you to think beyond the usual boundaries to discover their answers. When you do, you will be rewarded with wit and wisdom. When read with an open mind, not one fettered by opinions driven by ideology, you'll find E.O. is illuminating, amusing, captivating, and sometimes motivational, as he addresses the nuances of our everyday existence.

As he studied many world leaders' behaviours and the deceit in their political narratives, he found himself a rare breed on the political landscape. He knew of no one able to monopolise ideas, so he sought the opinion of others in a transparent way, which endeared the people to him. If we see despair in "The Unstableness of Things", there is hope in "Fragments of the Dawn, Part I" and motivation in "To the Ambitious Youth". "Vade Mecum" rewards us with a transcendental ambivalent introspection of the anthologist.

Most of E.O.'s poems were written before he entered the political arena, so we should not opine that his writings were motivated by political happenstance. If his poems show empathy, it is because he saw himself in the lives of the people around him; if we opine anger, it is because he was eager to see his country cut the umbilical cord of colonialism. E.O., a poor "country boy" as his opponents called him, became the leader of his people, as Chief Minister and subsequently as their first Premier.

In his later life, the author penned two particularly reflective and highly philosophical poems in Kwéyòl (Dominica dialect) with English translations. "Nomn Nwè" and "Cièck La Vie" serve as profound messages, not only to the country that revered him as their leader but also because they carry universal appeal, offering wisdom and insight to all readers.

Gabriel A. LeBlanc
Author's brother

ACKNOWLEDGEMENTS

This book is more than a collection of words; it is a tribute to the enduring legacy of our father, Edward Oliver LeBlanc. The process of compiling his poetic works has been both meaningful and rewarding. I am especially grateful to have shared this experience with my siblings—Erin, Einstar, Earlsworth, and Eustace. With the steadfast support of our families, we have worked together to preserve his voice and vision, ensuring that his story continues to resonate.

To my sister and brothers: thank you for your collaboration, patience, and commitment. Each of you contributed something essential to this project, and it was through our collective effort that we were able to complete what our father began.

We are grateful to our cousin Patricia David, as well as to Alick Lazare and Stacey Aaronson, for their generous guidance throughout the publishing process. To the exceptionally talented Aaron Hamilton: your distinctive style and artistic vision brought the final cover to life, beautifully capturing a landscape our father cherished. We are also thankful to Professor Karen Santry (New York University) for her artistic insight and original design concepts, which added depth to the creative process.

Special thanks go to Gregory Rabess for his meticulous editing of the Kwéyòl versions of "Nomn

Nwè" and "Cièck La Vie", and for his work in applying standard orthography throughout the translations. To Giselle Laurent: your expertise in pre-press production was essential to completing this book. We could not have done it without you.

Finally, we extend our deepest appreciation to all those who continue to preserve and celebrate the legacy of Edward O. LeBlanc, through scholarship, art, media, and community initiatives. Your work ensures that his influence remains a source of inspiration for generations to come.

Ewart LeBlanc
Author's son

www.ingramcontent.com/pod-product-compliance
Lightning Source LLC
Chambersburg PA
CBHW052042280426
43661CB00085B/39